Editor-in-Chief and Founder:
  Lyndon H. LaRouche, Jr.
Editorial Board: *Lyndon H. LaRouche, Jr. , Helga
  Zepp-LaRouche, Robert Ingraham, Tony
  Papert, Gerald Rose, Dennis Small, Jeffrey
  Steinberg, William Wertz*
Co-Editors: *Robert Ingraham, Tony Papert*
Managing Editor: *Nancy Spannaus*
Technology: *Marsha Freeman*
Books: *Katherine Notley*
Ebooks: *Richard Burden*
Graphics: *Alan Yue*
Photos: *Stuart Lewis*
Circulation Manager: *Stanley Ezrol*

INTELLIGENCE DIRECTORS
Counterintelligence: *Jeffrey Steinberg, Michele
  Steinberg*
Economics: *John Hoefle, Marcia Merry Baker,
  Paul Gallagher*
History: *Anton Chaitkin*
Ibero-America: *Dennis Small*
Russia and Eastern Europe: *Rachel Douglas*
United States: *Debra Freeman*

INTERNATIONAL BUREAUS
Bogotá: *Miriam Redondo*
Berlin: *Rainer Apel*
Copenhagen: *Tom Gillesberg*
Houston: *Harley Schlanger*
Lima: *Sara Madueño*
Melbourne: *Robert Barwick*
Mexico City: *Gerardo Castilleja Chávez*
New Delhi: *Ramtanu Maitra*
Paris: *Christine Bierre*
Stockholm: *Ulf Sandmark*
United Nations, N.Y.C.: *Leni Rubinstein*
Washington, D.C.: *William Jones*
Wiesbaden: *Göran Haglund*

ON THE WEB
e-mail: eirns@larouchepub.com
www.larouchepub.com
www.executiveintelligencereview.com
www.larouchepub.com/eiw
Webmaster: *John Sigerson*
Assistant Webmaster: *George Hollis*
Editor, Arabic-language edition: *Hussein Askary*

EIR (ISSN 0273-6314) *is published weekly
(50 issues), by EIR News Service, Inc.,
P.O. Box 17390, Washington, D.C. 20041-0390.
(703) 777-9451 ext. 415*

European Headquarters: E.I.R. GmbH, Postfach
Bahnstrasse 9a, D-65205, Wiesbaden, Germany
Tel: 49-611-73650
Homepage: http://www.eirna.com
e-mail: eirna@eirna.com
Director: Georg Neudecker

Montreal, Canada: 514-461-1557

Denmark: EIR - Danmark, Sankt Knuds Vej 11,
basement left, DK-1903 Frederiksberg, Denmark.
Tel.: +45 35 43 60 40, Fax: +45 35 43 87 57. e-mail:
eirdk@hotmail.com.

Mexico City: EIR, Sor Juana Inés de la Cruz 242-2
Col. Agricultura C.P. 11360
Delegación M. Hidalgo, México D.F.
Tel. (5525) 5318-2301
eirmexico@gmail.com

The Opportunity For a New Start

EIR Contents

www.larouchepub.com Volume 43, Number 47, November 18, 2016

Cover This Week

Boys in a Pasture, *Winslow Homer,* 1874

wikimedia

I. A Turning Point in History

Act Now to Seize the Opportunity Created by This Election!

EIR's Tony Papert interviewed Helga Zepp-LaRouche on Nov. 13.

EIR: Helga Zepp-LaRouche has long been on the international stage. She's the founder of the international Schiller Institute, a prestigious and influential international think tank. She's the leader of a German political party called Civil Rights Movement Solidarity. And she's known in China as the "Silk Road Lady" as an outcome of her and her husband Lyndon LaRouche's pioneering back in the end of the 1980s and the beginning of the 1990s, of the concept of the Eurasian Land-Bridge, which is now embodied in the Chinese government's policy called "One Belt, One Road," involving more than 100 countries internationally.

Helga, as a leader of Germany and also an international leader, what does Donald Trump's election last Tuesday mean for the world?

Helga Zepp-LaRouche: Well, I think the single most important effect is that it interrupted a very dangerously advanced drive towards World War III. If Hillary had been elected and become the new President, and followed through on what she said her policy on Syria would be—the no-fly zone, the anti-Russia, anti-China positions—an escalation to global thermonuclear war would have been almost certain. And that has been absolutely interrupted—not completely eliminated, because now the changes which have been created through this interruption have to be used. But look at the reactions of President Putin and many other in-

Helga Zepp-LaRouche

fluential people in Russia who all have expressed great hope that a real reset of Russian-U.S. relations would be possible. Putin stressed that he doesn't think it will be an easy task, given the fact that the U.S.-Russian relations have reached such an absolute low-point, but that it can be done. Without the restoration of the relationship between the United States and Russia and the United States and China, no other policy around the globe can function.

Therefore, I think that is the single most important outcome of this election. I think what has to occur now, is that all of the axioms associated with globalization, such as the new liberal monetary policies; the "right to protect," i.e. interference under the pretext of humanitarian interventions around the globe; the export of "democracy," and similar things; all of that has to stop. It has to be replaced by a completely new set of international relations. Models for that already exist in approximation. For example, China's President Xi Jinping has proposed for the past three years, especially to the United States, a new model for the relations among great powers, based on total respect for the sovereignty of the other nation; non-interference; respect for the different social system of the other country; and "win-win" cooperation for the mutual benefit of all. So, that is one starting point; and I think the principles of the UN Charter also have to be completely reinstated and revived.

EIR: It's been remarkable to me, how some of the German responses to this election have been very

Construction work at the Tennessee Valley Authority's Douglas Dam, 1942.

Library of Congress

unique and far-sighted; at least compared to anything else I've heard from the U.S. or from elsewhere in the world. I know you've discussed the same thing in more depth. Would you like to say anything about it?

Zepp-LaRouche: Unfortunately, that has not been the reaction of all Germans. You had, for example, the noteworthy reaction of German Defense Minister Ursula von der Leyen, who the morning after the election said she was totally shocked about the outcome—and this is the typical reaction for those people belonging to the establishment who have completely missed the significance of an earlier anti-establishment vote in the form of the Brexit in Great Britain, and now in the form of the Trump victory in the United States,—who have completely missed the point. Who are both completely out of reality and have no empathy for the victims of their own neo-liberal imperial policies. But as you said, that was not the only reaction in Germany, but I just

want to state for the record that that reaction is also there.

However, there were many other people, like the former chief of the Bundeswehr and high-ranking NATO official Harald Kujat, who stressed the absolute importance of restoring the U.S.-Russia relations. Then you have, remarkably, even in *Spiegel* which is a mainstream media,—but even there, you had a remarkable article saying that the only possible reaction in Germany and in Europe should be—in order not to repeat the mistakes of the 1930s, which led to the rise of Hitler, Mussolini, and so forth—would be that Germany at this point, and Europe, should go for an FDR solution, a New Deal. Then he elaborated the three phases of the New Deal— how Roosevelt got the United States out of the Depression. Now, that is excellent and that is exactly what should be done. I think that is the kind of discussion which is also very productive for the United States.

EIR: Since the election, your husband Lyndon La-

German high-speed rail: The first generation Intercity Express trains criss-cross the country, much like the TGV in France.

Rouche has referred several times to Germany's essential role in the new international system which has to be created, encompassing the World Land-Bridge program of China, also joined by Russia and India and major countries in Eurasia. I wondered if you could talk to us about the role of Germany in the new world system which has to be created in the present and the future.

Zepp-LaRouche: Well, the fortunate news is that this new world system is already in existence; even if it has not been covered by the mainstream media. In the last three years, since President Xi Jinping announced the New Silk Road and Maritime Silk Road of the 21st Century, the largest infrastructure program in the history of the world has already become a reality. It is already 12 times bigger in today's buying power than the Marshall Plan was. Already it involves 4.4 billion people; it involves 100 nations and large organizations; it involves huge corridors, power grids, nuclear cooperation, high-tech cooperation, among all of these nations. It involves a whole, completely new parallel financial system, which is completely devoted to investment in the real economy and not to casino speculation. So that system is already a reality; and Germany, obviously, with its specific characteristics of having a very highly developed *Mittelstand* (medium and small industry), where 85% of the patents are still being generated, has exactly the kind of machine-tool design capability and scientific and engineering knowledge, which is exactly what is needed for the reconstruction of the world economy. The German Development Minister, Gerd Müller, just announced that in the coming weeks, Germany will announce a Marshall Plan for Africa,— although the sum of 1 billion euro being mentioned is actually much to small. But I have proposed for a very long time that Germany and China should work together in the development of the African continent. Extend the Silk Road to Africa; and in that way create the only solution for the still-horrendous refugee crisis. I think if Mr. Trump really wants to quiet all the critics of his policy, the best way would be if he embarked—together with Russia and China, and Germany and other European countries—to reconstruct the

YouTube/DW

German Development Minister Gerd Müller at South Sudan refugee camp.

war-torn regions of the Middle East. I think that that would really put the world on a completely different trajectory, and would really change the world for the better right away.

EIR: Lyndon LaRouche has recently insisted on what he calls the increase of physical productivity as the touchstone for world and U.S. policy, and he's also said it's a difficult issue for many to understand. For instance, he said it's a difficult concept for U.S. Congressmen to understand. In the context of our discussion, I wonder if you could help our readers increase their understanding of the concept of the increase of physical productivity as the required direction of the economy?

Zepp-LaRouche: Fortunately, the free-trade agreements, the TPP and TTIP, are completely dead; and that's a good thing, because free trade does absolutely nothing to increase the productivity of the labor force. It's based on the monetarist conception of buying cheap and selling dear; it's based on the out-sourcing of cheap labor to slave labor markets, and it is exactly what strangles the increase of productivity by cementing the conditions of maximum profit at the expense of the labor force. On the other side, if one looks at those models of economy which always were the basis of the increase of the wealth of the population,—what Friedrich List, the German economist, characterized as the American System of economy, which he contrasted with the English system of economy—there the correct assumption is that the only source of wealth is the creativity of the population. This creativity, which takes the form of scientific and technological discoveries, is transformed into technological progress which, if applied in the production process, then leads to an increase of productivity of both the labor force and the industrial capacity. That is the only source of true wealth.

Now, that model of economy was the basis not only for Alexander Hamilton and the creation of the United States;

German-American economist Friedrich List

Wilhelm von Kardoff in 1903

it was the basis for Lincoln's economic measures like the greenback policy; and it was exactly the policy of Franklin D. Roosevelt and the New Deal. Many people don't know that it also was the basis of the transformation of Germany from a feudal state during the time of Bismarck into an industrial powerhouse, when that same Listian system was applied, and also the ideas of the economic advisor of Lincoln—Henry C. Carey—were made known in Germany, and caused Bismarck to change to go in this direction. There is a beautiful little book which I want to emphasize, which was written by a friend of Bismarck, Wilhelm von Kardoff. The title is *Against the Stream—Gegen den Strom*, where he describes in the clearest terms the difference between the non-functioning free-market/free-trade model, and the model of the American System of economy. I would really advise people to re-read these basic writings.

EIR: And my final question is—it seems to me, and you have more in-depth knowledge of it—that the history of German culture in the broad sense from Nicholas of Cusa and J.S. Bach, is central to Germany's role in solving the problems of humanity as a whole. It's something you've been occupied with for decades—I wonder if it's something you want to address in conclusion?

Zepp-LaRouche: Germany used to be called in the past the country of poets, philosophers, and inventors. Unfortunately, that very rich tradition has been replaced for the most part by the axioms of globalization and every distortion of knowledge which goes along with that. But fortunately, this tradition can be rediscovered; there can be a renaissance of the ideas associated in science with Nicholas of Cusa, Kepler, Leibniz, Riemann, and Einstein. In music, the Classical tradition of Bach, Beethoven, Schumann, and if I may include the Austrian composers Mozart and Schubert, and also naturally Brahms, who have long ceased to be German, but have become part of world Classical music. And in poetry and drama, the tradition of Lessing, Mendelssohn, Schiller,—and I would like to add the brothers Wilhelm and Alexander von Humboldt, who had an image of man which was really the most noble humanist conception. The idea that every human being can become and develop a beautiful character. Schiller said that every human being can become a beautiful soul; and he defined only the person who has that characteristic to be a genius. So, with the Wilhelm von Humboldt education system, the idea that every human being can become a genius is exactly what is in reach if we reach this new epoch of mankind, which is already on the horizon.

EIR: Terrific, wonderful! Great talking to you.

Germany Must Embrace The New Silk Road Initiative

by Helga Zepp-LaRouche, chairwoman of the German political party
Civil Rights Movement Solidarity (BüSo)

Nov. 12—The reason the forecasts of the establishment media and politicians about the U.S. presidential election were so totally off-base—as they were on the Brexit referendum—is obvious: All of the so-called experts and establishment figures who expressed their utter shock "the morning after"—such as our Defense Minister, Mrs. Ursula von der Leyen)—have long since lost contact with the actual processes going on in the population, and have lost any empathy with the victims of their neoliberal policies.

During the last phase of the campaign, Trump focussed on two themes that tipped the balance. He stressed (1) that Hillary Clinton's policy in Syria was leading to a nuclear war with Russia, and (2) that Roosevelt's Glass-Steagall banking separation law must be immediately reintroduced, an action which would bring an end to the casino economy of Wall Street. In this way he struck a chord especially with the population of the Rust Belt states of the Midwest, the former industrial centers that have been reduced to ruins. Consequently the people living there, who no longer see a future for themselves, have developed a deep-seated hatred for the power elite that lets Wall Street speculators make megagains, while they don't even have enough for the bare necessities.

The extraordinary arrogance with which the incorrigible representatives of neoliberal globalization—such as

Defense Minister von der Leyen, EU Commission President Jean-Claude Juncker, and *Bildzeitung* scribbler Franz Josef Wagner—thought it necessary to openly reprimand Trump after his election as President of the United States, reflects an unhealthy mixture of chutzpah and dissociation from reality. The defeat of Hillary Clinton, her just desserts for her clear intention to continue the policies of Bush, Cheney, and Obama, is the reflection of a global process.

It is, in a certain way, like the footfall of the chorus in Friedrich Schiller's poem "The Cranes of Ibykus": The voters were reminded of that higher power that, "judging, watches hid from sight." It is a clear rejection of the Anglo-American imperial policy which has brought the world to the edge of thermonuclear annihilation; the ripping-apart of the European Union, not

Albert Duce/CCBY-SA 3.0

In the American Rust Belt industrial center of Detroit, the western part of the abandoned Packard Automotive Plant.

least because of the refugee catastrophe; and a newly threatened financial chaos.

Crucial Course Corrections

Trump's victory has postponed the danger of world war for a short time. During this short interval, fundamental policy corrections must be made, otherwise instability everywhere will very soon threaten world peace anew.

As the first, most important step, the relationship between the United States and Russia must again be put on a reliable basis. President Putin, Russian economist Sergei Glazyev, and an entire array of other Russian officials, as well as important political figures in the West, have greeted Trump's election as an opportunity for the urgently needed new beginning between the two super-powers.

In reaction to Trump's election, Putin said: "Russia is ready to, and seeks a return to, full-format relations with the United States. Let me say again, we know that this will not be easy, but we are ready to take this road, take steps on our side, and do all we can to set Russian-U.S. relations back on a stable development track. This would benefit both the Russian and American peoples and would have a positive impact on the general climate in international affairs, given the particular responsibility that Russia and the U.S. share for maintaining global stability and security."

Trump himself announced he would visit Putin before he takes office. He will, however, have to deal with enormous resistance from the ranks of neocons in both political parties. Republican Party neocons did not support Trump during the election campaign, even when he was the frontrunner. But because so many forces throughout the world targeted Obama's war policy—and its threatened continuation by Hillary Clinton—the neocons in the United States are not the only forces who now are contending to determine the fate of the world, which can have no positive future unless there is a positive redefinition of U.S.-Russian relations.

The second necessary step—equally urgent—is the immediate passage of the Glass-Steagall law, before the currently threatened repeat of the 2008 financial crisis on an even greater and more catastrophic scale. The U.S. Congress will be back in Washington on Monday, November 14, and the Glass-Steagall law must be passed in this "lame duck" session. Glass-Steagall was included in the election platforms of both parties and is before both houses of Congress. It has 71 cosponsors in the House of Representatives. That is the only way to stop a new financial crash from triggering chaos at any point and bringing us back to the precipice of war before Trump moves into the White House.

Obviously, Wall Street and the City of London, along with their disciples in the EU, will attempt by all possible means to prevent the reintroduction of Glass-Steagall. But the financial oligarchy has already lost the battle for the Trans-Pacific Partnership (TPP) and the Transatlantic Trade and Investment Partnership (TTIP); it is thus far from being as invincible as some wimps may believe. If even *Der Spiegel* columnist Thomas Fricke can propose, in a very unusual article for *Der Spiegel*, that Europe must now enact a Rooseveltian New Deal if it wants to prevent a repetition of the 1930s, then even a representative of the "quality press" has the door open just a crack for the fresh air of clear thinking to come in.

Bremen Landesbank chief economist Folker Hell-meyer also expressed himself clearly in the *Wirtschafts-nachrichten* (Economic News), in identifying Trump's election as not only a risk, but "an extraordinary opportunity," he wrote, to redefine European foreign policy. China's "One Belt One Road" initiative right now offers an enormous opportunity for the "hidden champions" of the German *Mittelstand* (small and medium-sized industry). The future lies in the developing countries, which represent more than 62% of the world economy and 85% of the world's population, and are growing at an annual rate of 4 to 5.5%. The moment to build a land bridge between Lisbon, Vladivostok, Beijing, and New Delhi is now, he concluded, and then there would be no need to fear for Europe's future.

We Must Rise to a New Level

Lyndon LaRouche has stressed that an absolutely essential precondition for solving the strategic crisis is the raising of international relations to a completely new level.

The starting point for the discussion of such a new state of international relations must be the principles of the UN Charter, as well as President Xi Jinping's guidelines for redefining relations among the major nations—which he has proposed to the United States—and the principles that should be the basis for cooperation among nations participating in the building of the Silk Road, namely, absolute respect for the sovereignty of the other, no interference in others' internal affairs, re-

1

Glass-Steagall

Franklin D. Roosevelt signs Glass-Steagall Act, 1933.
National Archives

2

National Banking Credit Creation

First National Bank of the United States, Philadelphia.
Library of Congress

3

International Credit System

Chinese-funded railway construction in Kenya.
beyase.com

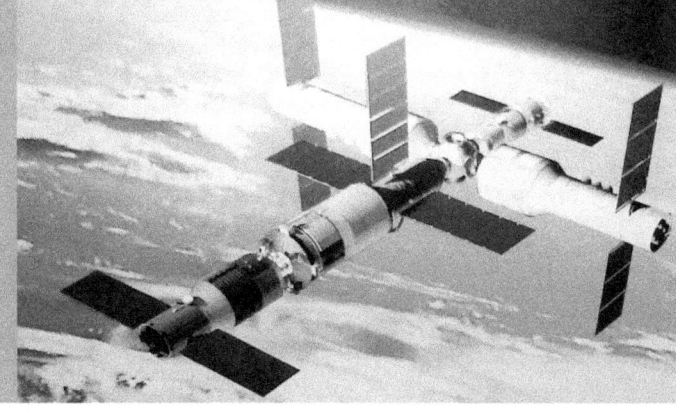

4

Science Driver

An artist's rendition of China's planned space station.
China.org

spect for different social systems, and a foreign policy based on mutual interests.

The four laws that Lyndon LaRouche has proposed for the reorganization of the world economy, imbue these principles with economic content: (1) the global enactment of Glass-Steagall laws; (2) the creation of a national bank in the tradition of Alexander Hamilton in every country; (3) the realization of an international credit system, a New Bretton Woods system; and (4) international cooperation in future-oriented scientific and technological fields, especially nuclear fusion and space exploration, to boost the productivity of the workforce.

To achieve the necessary new paradigm, which the nations of the world must agree on, we must prioritize the common aims of mankind over any national interest, as well as the dialogue of cultures from the standpoint of the best that each culture has created. Only if we can define and live by the principles flowing from such a Renaissance—principles consistent with the identity of mankind as a creative species—will we overcome the existential danger with which we are now faced.

Development Minister Gerd Müller's proposed Marshall Plan of a billion euro is a step in the right direction, but it falls far short. Germany can make a unique contribution to the necessary epochal change by officially declaring its cooperation with China's New Silk Road, especially in the reconstruction of the Middle East and the industrialization of Africa.

Every Day Counts In Today's Showdown To Save Civilization

That's why you need EIR's **Daily Alert Service**, a strategic overview compiled with the input of Lyndon LaRouche, and delivered to your email 5 days a week.

For example: On Oct. 28, EIR's Daily Alert highlighted the speech of Russian President Putin at the Valdai Club, where he put forth a series of economic initiatives, arguing that peace cannot be achieved without economic progress. This, despite all the filthy provocations being circulated against Russia in the Western press. Russia wants to cooperate economically as well as against terror.

The same edition also features the latest motion in the U.S. toward Glass-Steagall by, of all people, Donald Trump.

We're not just warning of the real dangers of financial collapse and war. Each edition of EIR Alert points to aspects of the rapid momentum toward sanity worldwide, providing information you need to act on if we are going to survive as a nation and a species. Can you really afford to be without it?

TUESDAY, NOVEMBER 1, 2016
Volume 3, Number 50

EIR Daily Alert Service

P.O. Box 17390, Washington, DC 20041-0390

- Hillary's Plan for Regime Change in Syria Means Nuclear War with Russia
- The Empire's Financial Times Gives 'Kiss of Death' Endorsement to Hillary Clinton
- Another Black Eye for Obama's Pivot to Asia, and War— Malaysia's Najib Visits China
- China, Philippines 'Friendly Understanding' Now Official on Fishing in 'Traditional' Areas
- Fidel Ramos Quits as Philippine Special Envoy to China
- UN's Syria Envoy Charges Jihadists with War Crimes in Eastern Aleppo

EDITORIAL

Hillary's Plan for Regime Change in Syria Means Nuclear War with Russia

Oct. 31 (EIRNS)—One thing that Donald Trump has correct is that

---

II. The Infinite Mind of Man

'Reconcile the total world! Seek above the stars unfurled!'

by Will Wertz

Will Wertz, President of the Schiller Institute, delivered the following remarks to celebrations of Friedrich Schiller's birthday on November 12, 2016. Wertz, a long time leading collaborator of Lyndon and Helga LaRouche, is the translator and editor of four volumes of Schiller's works into English.

Hello, my name is Will Wertz. I have the privilege of being the President of the Schiller Institute, which was founded by Helga Zepp-LaRouche back in 1984. I think we all owe a debt of gratitude to Helga for having introduced us to Friedrich Schiller and for having founded the Schiller Institute, which has increasingly, over the last decades, played a crucial role internationally in the efforts to create a new, just world economic order.

What I want to do today is to indicate the significance of Friedrich Schiller to the world as we face it. One of the most important things that Schiller developed was the need to educate man's emotions. He came to the conclusion that that was necessary following the French Revolution, where a great moment found a small-minded people who were easily manipulated, and instead of enjoying political freedom following the American Revolution, the French Revolution led to a massive catastrophe. The liberation of Europe from the oligarchy at that time did not occur.

We Cannot Be Mere Earthlings

One of the things that Friedrich Schiller writes in his Letters on the Aesthetical Education of Man, is that one should give the direction to the world of the good. He argues that although we live in our century, we should not be the creatures of our century; that what we need to give to humanity is what humanity needs, not what humanity praises. I think this is particularly appropriate to the circumstances we face today, in which there is an opportunity to shape the future, but it is an opportunity which we must seize very rapidly. The only way we can seize the future is by operating on a much higher plane than most people do, and, specifically what I would suggest, and this is based upon comments by Lyndon LaRouche on Wednesday and then also Thursday, is that, just as Schiller said, we have to live in our century but not be its creature, and give mankind what he needs, not what he praises. Similarly, even though we live on this planet, earth, we cannot be mere earthlings, that we have to locate our identity in terms of man's actual mission, and we have to organize humanity to recognize that mission and what true humanity represents.

That means, very concretely, that you have to place yourself outside of the earth. You have to, in a certain sense, locate yourself on the moon, or, in the short term, in the International Space Station, and that is the way you have to look at what is required on earth. This is what Krafft Ehricke argued in his writings on the extraterrestrial imperative. Similarly, what we have to do is move forward on a global basis to put together a new world economic order. The Russians, the Chinese, the Indians, the other BRICS nations have taken the initiative in this respect, but we have a world which is divided,

CC0
Friedrich Schiller, by Louis Ammy Blanc, 1861

with the trans-Atlantic region which is completely bankrupt, and it is absolutely necessary that we bring the United States into that geometry, economically. That is a big task, and it is one that can only be realized to the extent that throughout the world, people master the economic ideas of Alexander Hamilton and of Lyndon LaRouche's Four Laws.

There is a poem by Schiller, a very famous poem set to music by Beethoven, the Ode to Joy, set to music by Beethoven in the Ninth Symphony, in terms of this idea of placing oneself in the universe, which is what mankind's mission is, to master the universe. What Schiller does in all of his refrains is to place man in that position. For instance, "Brothers, o'er the stars unfurled, God doth judge as we have settled," or, further, "o'er the tent of stars unfurled, God rewards you from the heavens." That is the location, the placement which we must have if we are to address the needs of humanity at this point, and to ensure that the possibility of avoiding the destruction of humanity through thermonuclear war is fully realized, because, as Lyndon LaRouche has emphasized, as long as the financial conditions which have led the world to the point of war have not been resolved, then that war potential will continue to surface.

The Good Samaritan

Now, what I would like to do is point to a few of the most critical features of what Schiller elaborated. First of all, what he emphasized is that it is through beauty that man proceeds to freedom. You cannot have freedom unless, in fact, you have really created beautiful souls among humanity, which are characterized by the emotion of agape, which is Greek for love. That is the fundamental emotion, as Lyndon LaRouche has often called it, which is required. In many of Schiller's works, he deals with this fundamental issue and he says that if you actually operate from the standpoint of love, agape, love for the truth, love for humanity, you have entered into what he calls the joyous realm of play, of creative play, which is the actual nature of man.

In the Kallias letters, he discusses this in terms of his own version of the Good Samaritan parable from the Bible. He gives five examples of individuals who respond to a man who is wounded on the side of street. Only the fifth actually helps the individual without having a debate in his own mind as to whether he should do it. Many of the others, among other things, thought in terms of being paid for helping the person, and, what was in it for them. What Schiller argues is that the moral beauty arises only when duty has become nature to man. That is, you do your duty with joy, because your actual emotions are characterized by agape, by love.

In one of Schiller's writings, the Philosophical Letters, he writes, "When I hate, so I take something from myself; when I love, so become I so much the richer by what I love. Forgiveness is the recovery of an alienated property; hatred of man a prolonged suicide; egoism the highest poverty of a created being." He goes on to look at this from the standpoint of different conceptions of society. He writes, "Egoism and love separate mankind into two highly dissimilar races, whose boundaries never flow into one another. Egoism erects its center in itself; love plants it outside of itself, in the axis of the eternal whole. Love aims at unity; egoism is solitude. Love is the co-governing citizen of a blossoming free state; egoism a despot in a ravaged creation. Egoism sows for gratitude; love for ingratitude. Love gives; egoism lends."

Cancel the Debt

In other works of Schiller he develops the same concept. For instance, in the Legislation of Solon and Lycurgus, one of the first things that Solon did, when he became the leader of Athens—and replaced Draco, from whose name we derive the word draconian—one of the first things he did was to eliminate, to cancel the debt. What he did, as Schiller writes, "whereby all debts were annulled, and it was forbidden at the same time that in the future anyone be permitted to borrow on his own person." And you think of what is required in the trans-Atlantic sector at this point, which is full scale bankruptcy reorganization in which the debts are actually cancelled, just as Solon did previously. The alternative to that, as Schiller said, was the society in Sparta, which was based completely on slavery. Those are the alternatives which we still face to this day.

In On Universal History, one of Schiller's lectures he gave when he was a history professor, he writes the following. He distinguishes between the philosophical mind and the bread-fed scholar, the person who is just a careerist, just wants money. He talks about the philosophical mind: "He has always loved truth more than his system, and he will gladly exchange the old, insufficient form for a new one, more beautiful. Indeed, if no blow from the outside shatters his edifice of ideas, he himself will be the first to tear it apart, discontented, to re-establish it more perfected."

Discard the Failed System

That is love of truth; that is love of humanity: to throw away your previous beliefs and replace them with the truth on behalf of humanity, which is often something people are called upon to do at great moments in history, when failed systems must be discarded, failed systems of belief. That is the kind of moment we are in right now. In the French Revolution people did not discard the old system, and they faced their own destruction. That is the kind of situation we face today in the United States and throughout the world.

In one of his writings, called "The Artists," Schiller writes that this responsibility is really on the shoulders of the artist, and by implication we are all artists, because we all are in the image of the Composer of the universe. It applies not just to the person who identifies himself as an artist in a limited sense, but to all human beings. We should all function as artists, in terms of creating a more beautiful universe. What he says there is, "The dignity of man into your hands is given. Its keeper be. It sinks with you; with you it will be risen." That is an awesome sense of responsibility which every one of us must internalize and make one's own.

CC0

Statue of Friedrich Schiller, by Bertel Thorvaldsen, 1835

Hope

What I think I'll do is end with the following: we went through an election eight years ago which was all about hope and change, we were led to believe. But there is a real hope and there is a real basis for change. It's just that you have to actually develop your mind to understand what that is, so that you are not manipulated and made a fool. One of Schiller's most important poems is the poem, Hope, which ends with the following stanza:

> It is no empty fawning deceit,
>   Begot in the brain of a jester.
> Proclaimed aloud in the heart is it,
>   "We are born for that which is better."
> And what the innermost voice conveys,
>   The hoping spirit ne'er that betrays.

And I would maintain that that hope is based upon creating an aesthetical state of mind, freeing oneself from prejudices, freeing oneself from the conditions which otherwise condition the way you react, the way you behave; and rising to a level of creative play, in which you locate, you place your identity in the universe. I would say that that is precisely what Lyndon and Helga La-Rouche have emphasized over the decades and most recently in the last couple of days. That is the challenge for all of us; that is the challenge we have as we celebrate the 257th birthday of Friedrich Schiller. Also this weekend is the birthday of Sun Yat Sen, an individual who was very much influenced by the American Revolution.

In the "Wilhelm Tell" play—and I understand that at least in Texas there will be scenes performed from that— the play ends with one of the characters, I think it is Rudenz, saying in the final line of the play, "and I proclaim that all my serfs are free." That play was written in 1805. It was written really in support of the American Revolution, because in it you have the famous Rütli Oath, and you have the speech in which is said, "No! There is a limit to the tyrant's power, and we have to reach up into the stars and seize our inalienable rights." That is the perspective we have to have today.

Freedom To Go Beyond Planet Earth

On November 24, 1984 the Schiller Institute adopted the Declaration of the Unalienable Rights of Man, based on the Declaration of Independence, rewritten to include all humanity. What Schiller did in 1805 was to support the American Revolution, but at the same time to anticipate the need for the Emancipation Proclamation by Lincoln. I would say today he anticipated the Four Freedoms of Roosevelt, and the need, as expressed by Krafft Ehricke, for man to have the freedom to go beyond the planet earth and realize his true humanity.

Again, I would like to express my personal gratitude to Helga Zepp-LaRouche for having introduced me, and our organization, and through that, people throughout America and elsewhere throughout the world, to Friedrich Schiller. I count him among one of my best friends, and I hope you do too. So, with that, again, I give you greetings in your celebrations of Schiller's Birthday.

SPACE IS THE KEY

Create a New System of Cooperation Among Nations!

by Kesha Rogers

Nov. 14—I would like to continue on the theme that I presented in last week's issue of *Executive Intelligence Review*, written before the conclusion of the U.S. Presidential election. In the article titled, "Restore Our National Mission for Scientific Progress," I stated that Lyndon LaRouche had defined the standards for economic progress in his four urgently needed laws to save the United States.[1] In referring to the need for increased productivity within a society and its economy, Mr. LaRouche makes this point: "The question in terms of economy involves not simply products capable of measurement as such, but rather involves the requirement of developing human minds in new ways that the human mind has ever fashioned to do it."

In the aftermath of the U.S. presidential election, LaRouche has called for defining a new set of international relations among peoples and nations. This is not a matter of politics or personalities as such: LaRouche declared, "You have to depend on the creation of a new system, not a Trump system, but a new system which will meet the requirements of the development of a true international system."

LaRouche went on to declare that the crucial problem we face today "is that we do not have a defined international system which will secure peace. It doesn't yet exist, and we've got to make it ... It's going to take a lot of work by people to do it, because it's not just doing it by name; the problem is to understand how that can work. This can be done. This can be done with the collaboration of some parts of the world as a whole. The overall picture is not going to be easy, but there are some connections which could be made early. But there is a lot to do to get [it] in the right way of success."

The American people do not yet understand what is required to bring about a new system of international

---

1. For an exposition of Lyndon LaRouche's Four Laws, see http://action.larouchepac.com/know_the_full_story/.

NASA

To bring about the creation of a new system of cooperation among nations, space science is key. Shown, Cape Canaveral's Launch Complex 39.

relations and what will ensure a truly peaceful existence for the productive and economic benefit of all people. It is not merely a matter of casting a vote and hoping that someone will do something good for you, or that the next guy won't be as bad as the one before.

The New System Coherent with the Four Laws

It is essential for this nation and the world today that a new form of international relations between nations and human beings be developed and established on a higher level, and with a higher level of commitment to the good of all peoples and all nations. The very ideas forming the principles of our republic included this: "We hold these truths to be self-evident, that all men are created equal, that they are endowed by their Creator with certain unalienable Rights, that among these are Life, Liberty, and the pursuit of Happiness." The principles defined in our Declaration of Independence concern the nature of man and were instrumental in the fight for the development of our republic. They were fundamental to the thinking of our nation's first Treasury Secretary, Alexander Hamilton, who was instrumental in crafting the Declaration of Independence and inspiring the Preamble to the Constitution.

But these principles, which must be reflected in the new system of international relations, must also be restored in what we do here in the United States. Americans have been denied access to that which is truly human. We must restore our commitment to all who have been disavowed and thrown on the scrap heap through the policies of the last two administrations, and by a failed party system that was more concerned with protecting a party and defending a candidate than looking out for the well being and higher interests of all of our people. It is time to end the compromise: Wall Street's casino economy of endless speculation must be ended now. LaRouche's four laws must be immediately implemented, starting with the immediate reinstatement of Glass-Steagall.

Space Science To Elevate the Mind

The United States must now commit itself to the new paradigm and new era of development and progress of LaRouche's four laws. The question is, therefore, can we look beyond the superficial differences and petty concerns that are used to divide people and commit ourselves to a restored national mission that every person is deserving of? Nothing will come without hard work and dedication, and a demand for solutions that will be in the interest of all.

President-elect Trump sent out a message to the people of this nation and the world by way of a tweet: "The forgotten man and woman will never be forgotten again. We will all come together as never before." His words will only hold true when solutions that Lyndon LaRouche has put forward are immediately implemented. First, Glass-Steagall must be enacted immediately. A national banking system must be established just as directed by Treasury Secretary Alexander Hamilton. And our economy must be restored through the immediate implementation of a science-driver fusion program as outlined in the fourth and subsuming law of LaRouche's four laws.

In a recent discussion with members of his leadership team, LaRouche declared, "Space science is the way that people have to operate, because space science incorporates the crucial elements which are lacking from other sources."

Speaking more broadly about the economic dimension of the cognitive development of the people, LaRouche added, "You've got to get into the mind of the present population—internationally and nationally; you have to get into the mind of that person who has no conception whatsoever of what that mind requires. You can do things which will prompt development, but it's chiefly local development and regional development. We've got to get mechanisms of international trade and agreements thereof, and that is what's required urgently, right now!"

The Will to Make Breakthroughs

We have continued to witness an increase in hatred and contempt for the policies which have dominated the country for the past 16 years; it grew even stronger with President Obama's implementation of his murderous, so-called cost-cutting healthcare policy and, most emphatically, the egregious cuts in our nation's manned Space Program. Meanwhile, Obama continued to bail out Wall Street. The momentum in the population that led to victory in my two primary campaigns for the U.S. House of Representatives, confirmed that the fight was much bigger than party politics.

Those victories were only possible because I campaigned for a renewed national mission for scientific and economic progress, as expressed in the vision of many of the greatest leaders our nation—leaders such as Abraham Lincoln, Franklin Roosevelt, John F. Kennedy, and yes, most emphatically, Lyndon LaRouche. LaRouche continues, to this day, to represent the principled approach to what is required for a new era of progress in the world. Many nations at this very moment are committed to implementing his policies and solutions.

It is the very same fight for principle, not party, that we saw in the override of President Obama's veto of the Justice Against Sponsors of Terrorism Act (JASTA), which passed with flying colors.

The fight to save the Space Program was—and continues to be—much bigger than Obama not wanting us to lead in the exploration of space or his turning our Space Program over to the private sector profit hogs. The Space Program is key to defining a new system of relations among nations. Cooperation in space development requires the elimination of all limits to growth. The development of space requires acting to advance the creative identity unique to all human beings. It is the will to discover and to expand our minds—the will to make new breakthroughs in understanding the universe—that will advance our conditions of life throughout the entire Solar system. That, as the late space pioneer Krafft Ehricke very poetically declared, is "man's extraterrestrial imperative."

As Ehricke envisioned it, "Our work in space will change Earth's present, closed-world environment into an open one, with access to vast space resources and other critically needed benefits that will greatly improve the lives of all people, and preserve Earth at its best—as man's home and garden for the maximum human future."[2] Ehricke was keenly aware of the cognitive and creative dimension of this great improvement in the lives of all people.

Larger Meaning of China's Space Leadership

This issue of the true identity of mankind as mankind—and the defense of the truly creative nature of the human mind—is the fundamental one. The rejection of this truly human identity was the evil behind Obama's dismantling of our Space Program and all of the egregious policies that stemmed from that. This destructive policy was perfectly consistent with his refusal to take up the offer to join with China in the development of the New Silk Road for the mutual benefit of all nations.

China is leading the way with its offer of win-win cooperation for the advancement of all nations through collaboration in building the New Silk Road and cooperation in the development of space. China is leading in space exploration with its rapidly accelerating lunar program

and the Sept. 15 launch of its new space lab, Tiangong-2.

China's leadership is especially recognized for its plan to land a spacecraft and rover on the Moon's far side, an undertaking that no other nation has yet attempted. But first, China is developing Chang'e 5 to land somewhere on the lunar near side by the end of 2017 and return soil samples to Earth, the first sample return since 1976. Then it will land a spacecraft and rover, Chang'e 4, on the Moon's far side, in 2018. If Chang'e 5 is successful, China could use the back-up craft built for that mission, for a proposed Chang'e 6, which could be used to collect and return the first far-side soil samples, according to Wu Yanhua, vice administrator of the China National Space Administration.

Meanwhile, the BRICS nations are attentive to China's leadership. The BRICS nations' space agencies have just concluded their first annual summit and have committed to many joint space initiatives for peaceful purposes, including a shared satellite system for earth remote sensing and communication. And the New Silk Road now involves 100 nations with a combined population of 4.4 billion people. They are also interested in a future in space.

Xi's Message to Trump

In the aftermath of the U.S. election, China's President Xi Jinping spoke by telephone with President-elect Donald Trump, proposing U.S.-China cooperation once again. Xi said, "The facts prove that cooperation is the only correct choice for China and the United States. The two sides must strengthen coordination, promote the two countries' economic development and global economic growth, expand all areas of exchange and cooperation, ensure the two countries' people obtain more tangible benefits, and push forward in China-U.S. relations."

That is exactly the cooperation that is needed to bring about the new system of international relations that LaRouche declares is urgently required.

To paraphrase Mr. LaRouche, the events that led to the results of the presidential election were not a matter of U.S. politics as such, but were rather global in scope and reflected a global need and a global process. We must act now to bring about a new system of international relations. As he states in the conclusion of his "Four New Laws" paper, "A Fusion economy, is the presently urgent next step, and standard, for man's gains of power within the Solar system, and, later, beyond." Cooperation in space exploration for the shared benefit of all nations will pave the way for a new system of international cooperation.

---

2. Krafft Ehricke, "Lunar Industrialization and Settlement—Birth of Polyglobal Civilization," in: W.W. Mendell (ed.), *Lunar Bases and Space Activities of the 21st Century* (Houston: Lunar and Planetary Institute, 1985), p. 827.

The Belt and Road Initiative and the Intercontinental Corridor of Infrastructure[1]

Review of *The New Silk Road Becomes the World Land-Bridge, EIR, 2014*

by Shi Ze

Since its inception in 2013 when Chinese President Xi Jinping visited Central Asia and Southeast Asia, the Belt and Road Initiative, namely the Silk Road Economic Belt and the 21st Century Maritime Silk Road, has received much attention both at home and abroad. With the progress of the Initiative and the emergence of early harvests, planning and research for the Belt and Road Initiative are now high on the agenda in China in different sectors and areas. However, the Initiative is far from mature in terms of related policies, and its further advance is in urgent need of in-

tellectual support. It is against this background that a report from Germany's Schiller Institute, The New Silk Road Becomes the World Land-Bridge, was published. Compared to most domestic reports that are still limited to introducing the situation and interpreting concepts, it is undoubtedly a weighty academic work of a type un-

1. Originally published in China International Studies, Jan./Feb. 2016, and reprinted by permission of the author.

Dr. Shi Ze is Senior Research Fellow and Director of the Center for International Energy Strategy Studies, China Institute of International Studies. He can be reached at shize@ciis.org.cn.

common in recent years.

The report will make substantial contributions to research on the Belt and Road Initiative. With a preface by Helga Zepp-LaRouche, the founder of the Schiller Institute, the report emphasizes the role that a "corridor of infrastructure" can play in driving national and regional economic development, and discusses the significance of initiatives such as the Belt and Road. With chapters written respectively by internationally prominent scholars and experts, the report analyzes the "corridors of infrastructure" of major countries and regions, and provides far-sighted and unique visions, which will be beneficial to the Belt and Road Initiative's realization of regional connectivity.

Three features of this report are particularly noteworthy. First, it puts an emphasis on the importance of abandoning a geopolitical mentality. According to the report, traditional geopolitical thinking, characterized by a zero-sum mentality, is the root of wars, poverty, starvation and desperation, and has repeatedly brought human civilization to the brink of crisis. For the sake of sustaining our civilization, the international community must abandon this obsolete mentality and establish the principles of mutual benefit and win-win cooperation as the new guides for our thinking and behavior.

On the one hand, by doing so, the sustainability of human beings, the only creative species on the globe, can be ensured. On the other hand, a healthy global atmosphere can be fostered to effectively tackle the common threats facing humankind.

Second, the large-scale construction of corridors of infrastructure is conducive to the creation of a new international economic order. From Lyndon LaRouche's criticism of free market-based monetarism, the report argues that this economic pattern, characterized by statistics and false algorithms, was the cause of the economic recession that has gripped the world since 2008. In response to the failure of this economic pattern, it is suggested that developing countries should enhance the construction of corridors of infrastructure, including railways, highways, waterways and aviation routes, in order to realize common development through the innovation of technology and the integration of resources both national and regional. Based on this understanding, the report specifically emphasizes that China's Belt and Road Initiative and reciprocal cooperation among BRICS countries are likely to shape a new international economic order, even a new developmental pattern beneficial to the sustainability of human civilization.

Third, the report explores in a concise way the intercontinental corridors with the potential for realizing connectivity. Promoting international and interregional connectivity of infrastructure is a critical part of the Belt and Road Initiative. In order to achieve this, besides clearly defining China's own current and planned infrastructure projects, it is necessary to understand comprehensively and deeply the related projects proposed by countries along the Belt and Road. So far, domestic academic and policymaking circles are still far behind in this respect, partly because the Initiative is still fresh and previous research inadequate. The publication of the report makes up for this. Displaying the current and planned corridors of infrastructure of major countries (China, Russia, the United States, and Germany, etc.) and regions (Eurasia, South and Central Asia, Southwest Asia, East and Southeast Asia, and Africa) through both text and illustrations, the report paves the way for further promotion of connectivity among the Belt and Road countries.

Besides these three features, it is commendable that the report reviews the introduction of the First and Second Eurasian Land Bridges, and discusses the position of major countries and regions within the network of intercontinental corridors of infrastructure. The report also provides some to-the-point solutions for important challenges, such as the exhaustion of water resources and expansion of nuclear energy use; and it elaborates skillfully and accurately on several professional issues related to the corridors of infrastructure.

The keynote of the report is optimistic. This optimism is based on its confidence in humans as the only creative species on the globe. It is farsighted as it accords with the general trend of human societal evolution. From this understanding, the report urges countries to abandon their geopolitical mentality and reshape a new global economic order. However, whether this vision can be realized remains uncertain. As is indicated in the ongoing Ukraine Crisis and the rivalry between the West and Russia around it, as well as the increasingly complicated interaction in the Asia-Pacific between China and the United States, traditional geopolitical thinking is yet to fade into history and still brings inevitable trouble to international cooperation. Given this, the realization of the Belt and Road Initiative and the connectivity of multiple corridors of infrastructure are not just economic and development issues, but also concern about security and politics. Regrettably, this report does not throw much light on how to tackle and prevent the negative effects of political and security factors, and we look forward to additional elaboration on these issues when the report is reprinted.

Madam Helga Zepp-LaRouche is a famous social activist and an expert in international studies well-known in China. Her understanding and anticipation of China's strategies deeply impressed me. Under Madam LaRouche's leadership, the Schiller Institute has become one of the first academic institutions to conduct research on the New Silk Road issues. Her speech two decades ago at a symposium on the Eurasian Land Bridge clearly outlined a vision of the New Silk Road, and put forward thought-provoking ideas and arguments. Therefore, the Schiller Institute's report and research into Belt and Road issues is not an overnight effort, but one based on longtime endeavors and reflections.

Generally speaking, *The Silk Road Becomes the World Land-Bridge* is an informative report with unique perspectives and constructive arguments. As China is actively materializing the Belt and Road Initiative, the report's Chinese version also bears practical significance and deserves our careful and in-depth study.

EDITORIAL

A New Conception of What International Relations Are

Lyndon LaRouche spoke as follows in discussion with associates on November 10.

"The whole economic system is not ready to work. We've got to get that system functioning, not just a few things here and there. We've got to pull [together] a special kind of organization which facilitates the ability of getting more parts of the world in the hands of the other part of the world. Otherwise, the thing won't work. You've got to pull things together. If you don't have a connection, you don't have a contract... What you're going to see on this question is a more complicated thing. What you're going to get is an understanding of a new conception of what international relations are. That's what is going to happen, and that's the way it will work. Otherwise, it will not work for obvious reasons, for those who are familiar with the details of the German and other economies.

"One of the problems is that there is presently no qualified content of developing the relations among these nations. You've got to get an actual content, which has to be functional. That's one of the things we have to work on, but that's not in place now.

"The problem is that we do not have a defined international system which will secure peace. It doesn't yet exist, and we've got to make it... It's going to take a lot of work by people to do it, because it's not just doing it by name; the problem is to understand *how* that can work. This can be done. This can be done with the collaboration of some parts of the world as a whole. The overall picture is not going to be easy, but there are some connections which could be made early. But there is a lot to do to get [it] in the right way of success.

"I wouldn't depend on Trump. He's going to do what he's going to do, but don't depend on him. You have to depend on the creation of a *new* system, not Trump's system but a new system, a global system which will meet the requirements of the development of a true international system. And you have to organize people on that basis. You cannot just say, 'We're going to try to make this thing work.' It won't work. It won't work. But we can start. I would say Germany,—Germany has a potential; if it wants to do so, it probably could make a good contribution... What Putin is doing is excellent, and it's well integrated; China is becoming very well integrated in many respects. You're getting development in parts of Asia. All these things are in place, but you've got to get the mechanism which makes it all come together in a syncretic way.

"Space science is the way that people have to operate, because space science incorporates the crucial elements which are lacking from other sources.

"You've got to get into the mind of the present population internationally and nationally; you have to get into the mind of that person who has no conception whatsoever of what that mind requires. What you can do is, you can do things which will prompt development, but its chiefly local development and regional development. We've got to get mechanisms of international trade and agreements thereof, and that's what's required urgently, right now!

"Odds and ends will not do this. So, therefore, don't try odds and ends. You've actually got to get into the gut of the mind of the people of different nations. I've had a lot of experience in this thing. It doesn't come out because of people who are not really understanding of what this is about, but looking in the course of history, you would say that I have a *very keen insight into humanity*. But not all the people in it are participating. That's the problem."

www.ingramcontent.com/pod-product-compliance
Lightning Source LLC
Chambersburg PA
CBHW051953280526
45789CB00009B/3278